Contents

D1240120

Practice Book

i

Use with *United States History*

Use with *United States History*

Name _____ Date _____

Almanac Map Practice

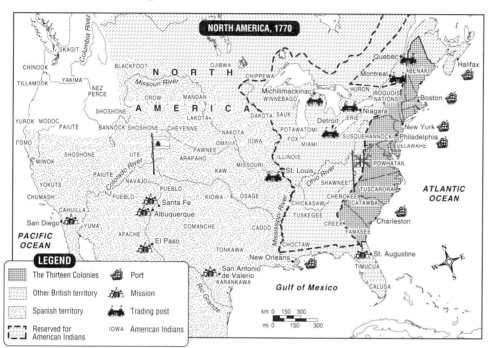

Use the map to do these activities and answer these questions.

Practice

1. Along which ocean is San Diego located? _____

2. Name three different American Indian groups that lived north of the

   Colorado River in Spanish territory. _____

   _____

   _____

3. Along which river are three missions located? _____

4. If a traveler headed directly north from New Orleans, what is the first

   American Indian group the traveler would likely meet? _____

Apply

5. With a partner, read the section "North America in 1500" in Chapter 2,
   Lesson 1. Describe how life was different for American Indian groups
   in 1500 compared to 1770.

_____

Almanac Graph Practice

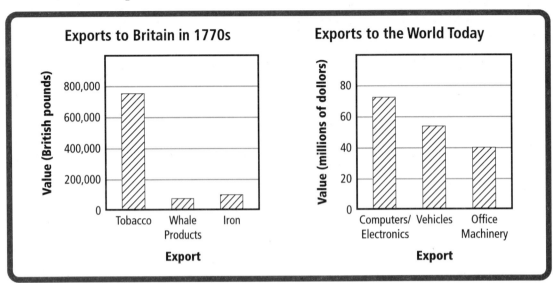

Exports to Britain in 1770s

Exports to the World Today

Practice

1. Which product did the United States sell the most of to Britain during

   the 1770s? _____

2. How many dollars worth of office machinery does the United States

   export to the world today? _____

Apply

3. Use the information below to complete the line graph.

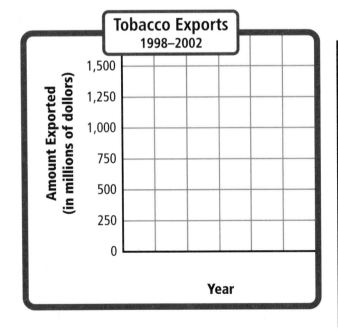

Tobacco Exports
1998–2002

Tobacco Exports, 1998–2002

Year	Amounts Exported (in millions of pounds)
1998	1,480
1999	1,293
2000	1,053
2001	992
2002	890

Vocabulary and Study Guide

Vocabulary

Write the definition of each vocabulary word below.

1. economic system _____

_____

2. resource _____

3. opportunity cost _____

_____

4. scarcity _____

5. Choose two words. Use each word in a sentence about the lesson.

_____

_____

Study Guide

Read "The Land and Its Resources." Then fill in the comparison chart below to compare natural, capital, and human resources.

	Natural resources	Capital resources	Human resources
What are some examples?	6.	7.	8.
What are they used for?	9.	10.	11.

Practice Book

3

Use with *United States History*, pp. 6–9

Name _____ Date _____

Skillbuilder: Review Map Skills

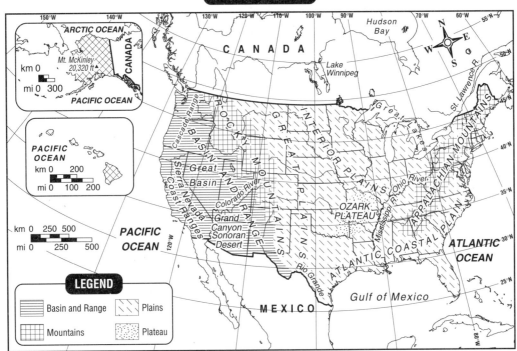

Practice

1. What is the title of this map? _____

2. How many miles is it from the Pacific Ocean to the Rocky Mountains?

   _____

3. At approximately what latitude and longitude is the southern end of
   Lake Michigan? Explain how you used the grid lines to locate the lake.

   _____

   _____

   _____

Apply

Look at the resources map in Lesson 1. How do the title, legend, and
labels change the information that the map gives?

   _____

   _____

   _____

4   Use with *United States History*, pp. 12–13

Vocabulary and Study Guide

Vocabulary

1. Draw a line connecting the vocabulary word to its meaning.

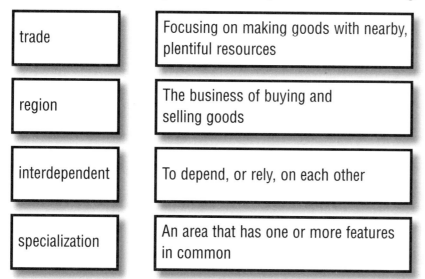

trade	Focusing on making goods with nearby, plentiful resources
region	The business of buying and selling goods
interdependent	To depend, or rely, on each other
specialization	An area that has one or more features in common

Study Guide

2. Read "What Is a Region?" Then fill in the blanks below.

One way to study regions in the United States is to group together _____ that are close to each other. Another way to study regions is by looking at similar _____. For example, the _____ region is made up of flat land and gently rolling hills. The United States is divided into climate regions such as the _____ region, which is hot and rainy.

3. Read "Regions and the Economy." Then fill in the blanks below.

Each region of the United States uses its _____ to produce goods and services. Georgia has the perfect climate for growing _____. Minnesota and _____ have a lot of iron ore. Farms and businesses _____ goods from one region to another. All of the regions of the United States are _____ because they depend, or rely, on each other.

Practice Book
5
Use with *United States History*, pp. 14–17

Vocabulary and Study Guide

Vocabulary

Solve the clue and write the answer in the blank. Then find the word in the puzzle. Look up, down, forward, and backward.

1. Anything that makes the water, air, or soil dirty and unhealthy
   _____

2. The surroundings in which people, plants, and animals live _____

3. A moist area such as a swamp or marsh _____

4. The protection and wise use of natural resources
   _____

5. A community of plants and animals, along with nonliving things _____

E	C	Y	I	H	X	R	F	A	S	O
P	O	L	L	U	T	I	O	N	V	C
L	N	F	H	E	U	N	T	I	K	T
J	S	G	N	T	S	Q	E	W	R	J
W	E	T	L	A	N	D	C	G	H	O
M	R	W	V	G	F	U	O	D	Q	K
Z	V	G	X	J	H	F	S	X	S	U
N	A	C	W	D	O	A	Y	J	L	B
A	T	M	E	I	Y	E	S	K	P	V
Q	I	D	Y	C	R	K	T	B	M	D
C	O	Z	L	B	P	A	E	Z	B	P
E	N	V	I	R	O	N	M	E	N	T

Study Guide

Read "People and the Environment." Then fill in the chart below.

How land affects people	How land changes	How people affect the environment
6.	7.	8.

Vocabulary and Study Guide

Vocabulary

Write the definition of each vocabulary word below.

1. agriculture _____

2. culture _____

3. migration _____

4. Choose two words. Use each word in a sentence about the lesson.

_____

_____

_____

Study Guide

5. Read "North America in 1500." Then fill in the outline below.

   I. Main Idea: American Indians developed different ways of life.

      A. Supporting Idea: The Great Plains Indians hunted buffalo.

         1. Detail: _____

         2. Detail: _____

           _____

      B. Supporting Idea: American Indians in the Southeast lived differently.

         1. Detail: _____

           _____

         2. Detail: _____

      C. Supporting Idea: American Indians in the Northwest and Southwest depended on the environment.

         1. Detail: _____

           _____

         2. Detail: _____

           _____

Vocabulary and Study Guide

Vocabulary

Across

1. A person who buys and sells goods to make money
2. The science of planning and guiding the route of a ship

Down

3. The movement of goods between Europe and the Americas is called the Columbian ——— .
4. A journey with an important goal
5. The money left over after expenses have been paid

Study Guide

Read "Europeans in America." Then fill in the explorer chart below.

Explorer	What did he do?
Vasco da Gama	6.
Christopher Columbus	7.
John Cabot	8.
Pedro Álvares Cabral	9.
Jacques Cartier	10.
Henry Hudson	11.

Vocabulary and Study Guide

Vocabulary

Use the vocabulary words in the box to fill in the word webs.

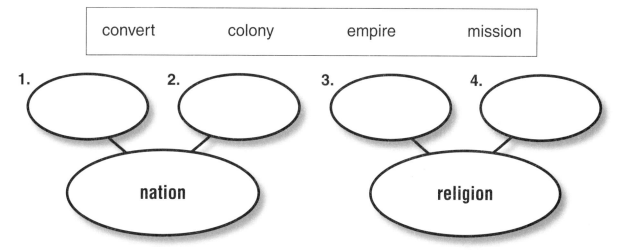

| convert | colony | empire | mission |

1.
2.
3.
4.

nation

religion

Study Guide

5. Read "New Spain." Then fill in the blanks below.

In 1519, the Spanish explorer _____ landed

on Aztec land. The Spanish wanted to find _____

and conquer the area. The Aztecs drove the Spanish away from

the capital city of _____. Cortés later defeated

the Aztecs and more Spanish came to the _____.

Catholic priests tried to convert the _____.

6. Read "Challenges to New Spain." Then fill in the blanks below.

Many other _____ wanted to explore and settle

in the Americas. _____ claimed an area in present-

day Canada for _____. The _____

claimed all the land along the Hudson River. They called this land

_____. In 1664, _____ ships

attacked this area. The English renamed New Amsterdam and called

it _____.

Vocabulary and Study Guide

Vocabulary

Write the word for each definition below.

1. Respecting beliefs and ways of acting that are different from your own

_____

2. A big farm on which crops are raised by workers who live there

_____

3. When the people who live in a place make laws for themselves

_____

4. A crop that is grown and sold to earn money _____

5. A person who owned and controlled all the land of a colony

_____

Study Guide

Read "Three Regions." Then fill in the comparison chart.

	What were the names of the colonies?	Why did colonists settle there?
New England	6.	7.
Middle Colonies	8.	9.
Southern Colonies	10.	11.

Use with *United States History*, pp. 50–55

Skillbuilder: Make a Timeline

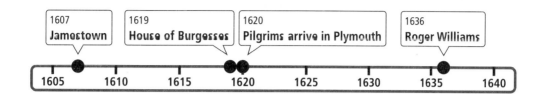

Practice

1. What is the span of years shown on the timeline? _____

2. What is the earliest date of an event on the timeline? _____

3. What is the latest date of an event on the timeline? _____

4. What is the difference in years between when Jamestown was

   founded and when the Pilgrims arrived in Plymouth? _____

Apply

Now you can make your own timeline about new settlements in North America. Read "New France" and "New Netherland" in Lesson 3. Write each date and what happened on each date. Put the dates in order. Complete the timeline.

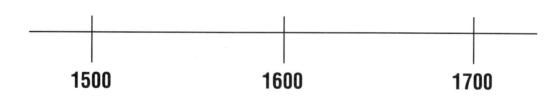

Almanac Map Practice

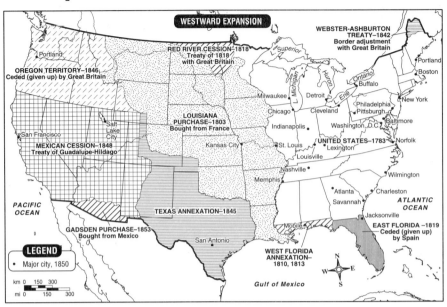

Use the map to do these activities and answer these questions.

Practice

1. In which region of the United States did Europeans first settle?

_____

2. Which became part of the United States first, West Florida or East

Florida? _____

3. Shade the area that the United States purchased from France.

4. What area was added to the United States in 1845?

_____

5. If a woman lived in San Francisco in 1823, was she living in the United

States? Why or why not? _____

_____

Apply

6. Work with a partner to locate the place where you currently live. Was
it added to the United States before or after 1783?

_____

_____

Almanac Graph Practice

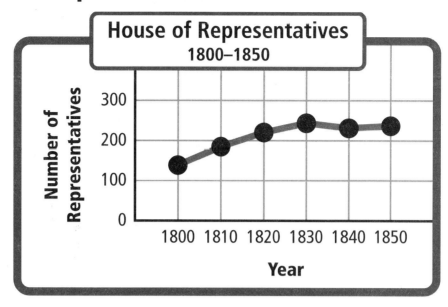

House of Representatives
1800–1850

Practice

1. In which year were there about 190 members of the House of

   Representatives? _____

2. During which ten-year period did membership in the House of

   Representatives decline? _____

Apply

3. Use the information below to complete the bar graph.

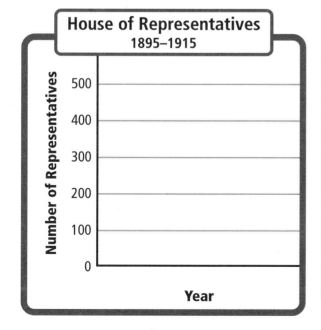

House of Representatives
1895–1915

House of Representatives, 1895–1915

Year	Number of Representatives
1895	357
1900	357
1905	386
1910	391
1915	435

Vocabulary and Study Guide

Vocabulary

Across
1. Freedom from being ruled by someone else
2. Freedoms protected by law

Down
3. An official gathering of people to make decisions
4. Money that citizens pay to their government for services
5. An overthrow or complete change of government

Study Guide

Read "Conflicts Begin." Then fill in the cause-and-effect chart below.

Causes		Effects
Parliament passes the Stamp Act.	6.	
Parliament passes the Tea Act.	7.	
Parliament passes laws to take power away from colonial governments.	8.	

Vocabulary and Study Guide

Vocabulary

1. Draw a line connecting the vocabulary word to its meaning.

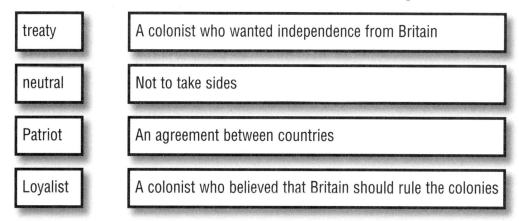

treaty	A colonist who wanted independence from Britain
neutral	Not to take sides
Patriot	An agreement between countries
Loyalist	A colonist who believed that Britain should rule the colonies

Study Guide

Read "Fighting the War." Then fill in the sequence chart below.

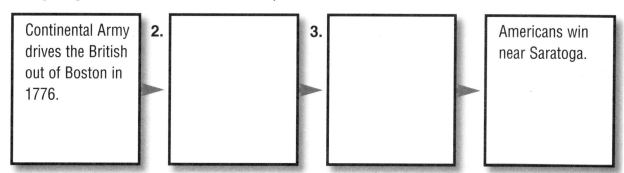

Continental Army drives the British out of Boston in 1776.	2.	3.	Americans win near Saratoga.

Read "Winning the War." Then fill in the sequence chart below.

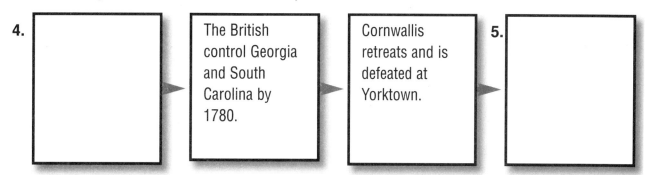

4.	The British control Georgia and South Carolina by 1780.	Cornwallis retreats and is defeated at Yorktown.	5.

Practice Book
15   Use with *United States History*, pp. 76–79

Skillbuilder: Make a Decision

Decision to be Made: How to make the United States government strong enough to keep order.

Option 1: Keep the Articles of Confederation

Consequences: States remain strong but government cannot keep order.

Option 2: Write a new constitution

Consequences: Government can keep order but may be too strong.

Final Decision: Write the Constitution, which gives the federal government more power but also limits what it can do.

Practice

1. What was the first option the delegates had?

_____

2. What decision did the delegates reach?

_____

3. Some delegates chose to vote for the Virginia Plan. Fill in a chart like the one above to show how a delegate might choose to vote for the Virginia Plan. What are the options? What are the consequences of each option? Complete your chart on a separate sheet of paper.

Apply

Use your decision-making skills to help Frank and Marcy settle a disagreement. Frank wants to watch a movie, and Marcy wants to play a game. Explain to them how they might make a decision together.

_____

_____

_____

Use with *United States History*, pp. 82–83

Vocabulary and Study Guide

Vocabulary

Solve the clue and write the answer in the blank. Then find the word in the puzzle. Look up, down, forward, and backward.

E	C	A	S	M	T	U	I	J	R
C	O	N	F	E	D	E	R	A	I
A	M	R	F	J	D	L	B	C	J
G	P	O	T	X	E	L	C	A	L
M	R	A	T	I	F	Y	F	N	A
T	O	P	I	H	E	D	J	V	R
U	M	Y	R	G	H	M	N	C	E
P	I	K	D	B	S	B	E	L	D
A	S	O	O	A	I	U	I	J	E
Z	E	T	A	G	E	L	E	D	F

1.	An agreement reached where each side gives up something that it wants
2.	Someone chosen to speak and act for others
3.	A system in which the national and the state governments divide and share power
4.	To officially accept a plan

Study Guide

Read "Articles of Confederation." Then fill in the compare-and-contrast chart below.

What the national government could do under the Articles	What the national government could not do
5.	**6.**

Vocabulary and Study Guide

Vocabulary

Solve the clue and write the answer in the blank. Then find the word in the puzzle. Look up, down, forward, and backward.

1.	A right to vote
2.	An official statement or position
3.	Interpreters _____ what is being said in different languages.
4.	The edge of a country or a settled area

S	U	F	F	R	A	G	E
A	O	R	G	U	N	N	T
F	R	O	N	T	I	E	R
I	E	C	D	R	A	N	Y
H	E	S	T	R	L	B	T
R	N	C	K	L	P	G	S
E	O	D	P	M	X	R	P
D	I	J	I	G	E	U	H

Study Guide

5. Read "Pioneers Cross the Appalachians" and "The Louisiana Purchase." Then fill in the blanks below.

Settlers wanted to cross the _____

because the land in the East was becoming crowded.

_____ built the Wilderness Road through the

_____, which allowed settlers to cross the

Appalachian Mountains. Later, President Jefferson purchased the

Louisiana Territory from France and sent Meriwether Lewis and

_____ to explore the new area.

6. Read "War of 1812." Then fill in the blanks below.

After the War of 1812, President Monroe issued a warning to

_____ about new colonization. This warning

is known as the _____. In 1828,

_____ for white men who did not own land

helped Andrew Jackson become President.

Vocabulary and Study Guide

Vocabulary

1. Use *interchangeable parts, mass production,* and *productivity* in one or two sentences that show their relationship.

   _____

   _____

   _____

2. Use *entrepreneur* and *textile* in a sentence that shows their relationship.

   _____

   _____

   _____

Study Guide

Read "The Industrial Revolution Begins." Then fill in the sequence chart below to show the main events in the history of the textile industry.

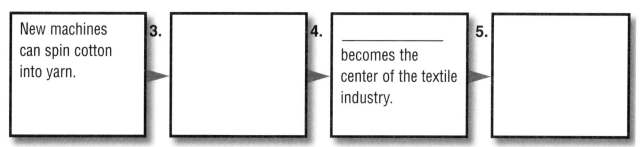

Read "Changes in Transportation." Then fill in the compare-and-contrast chart below to show how each change affected transportation.

National road	Canals and steamboats	Railroad
6.	7.	8.

Skillbuilder: Draw Conclusions

Meriwether Lewis and William Clark led an expedition to explore the land west of the Mississippi River. A Shoshone woman named Sacagawea joined their group as an interpreter. Sacagawea helped Lewis, Clark, and the other men in the group communicate with the American Indians they met. Sacagawea made it easier for these American Indian groups to trust Lewis and Clark.

Lewis and Clark kept journals describing the people and the land. They made a map of the rivers and mountains in the West. These details had never been shown on a map before. They found that it was possible to cross over the Rocky Mountains.

Practice

1. Name two facts about Sacagawea from the passage.

_____

_____

2. What can you conclude about Sacagawea from the passage?

_____

3. List two details that would support the following conclusion: The discoveries of Lewis and Clark would help future pioneers in the West.

_____

_____

Apply

Read "The Louisiana Purchase" in Lesson 1. Then write a paragraph to explain what you can conclude about President Jefferson based on the information you read. Support your paragraph with details from the lesson.

_____

_____

_____

_____

Use with *United States History*, pp. 120–121

Vocabulary and Study Guide

Vocabulary

1. Write the definition of *annexation*.

_____

2. Use *annexation* and *republic* in a sentence.

_____

_____

3. Write the definition of *boomtown*.

_____

4. Use *boomtown* and *forty-niner* in a sentence.

_____

_____

Study Guide

Read "Texas and the Mexican War." Then fill in the sequence chart below.

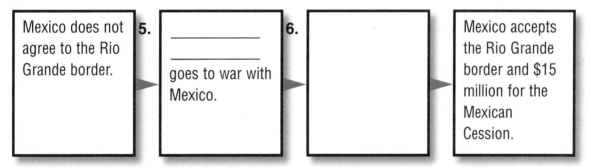

| Mexico does not agree to the Rio Grande border. | **5.** _____ _____ goes to war with Mexico. | **6.** | Mexico accepts the Rio Grande border and $15 million for the Mexican Cession. |

Read "Moving West." Then fill in the compare-and-contrast chart below to show some of the people who traveled to each territory and why.

Oregon Territory	California
7.	**8.**

Almanac Map Practice

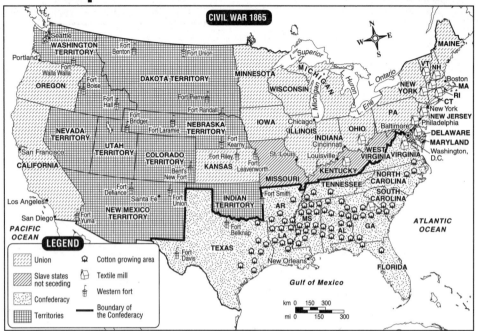

Use the map to do these activities and answer these questions.

Practice

1. Draw a circle around each major city in both the Union and Confederacy.

2. How many major cities does the map show on the Union side? The

   Confederate side? _____

3. On which side of the Civil War were most cotton producers located?

   Most textile mills? _____

   _____

Apply

4. Work with a partner. Read about free states and slave states in "Compromises in Congress" in Lesson 3 of Chapter 12.

   Look at the map above. Then explain why Missouri was a slave state, Maine was a free state, and Kansas and Nebraska were given popular sovereignty.

   _____

   _____

Almanac Graph Practice

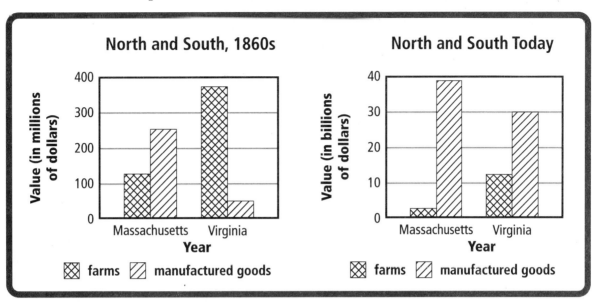

North and South, 1860s

Value (in millions of dollars) / Massachusetts / Virginia / Year
farms / manufactured goods

North and South Today

Value (in billions of dollars) / Massachusetts / Virginia / Year
farms / manufactured goods

Practice

1. In the 1860s, did southern states such as Virginia rely more on

farming or manufacturing? _____

2. About how many billions of dollars of manufactured goods does

Massachusetts produce today? _____

Apply

3. The information in the chart compares the amount of money people earned in Massachusetts and Virginia in 1950 and 2000. Use the data in the chart to complete the double bar graph below.

Personal Income Per Person

State	1950	2000
Massachusetts	1,656	37,960
Virginia	1,257	31,320

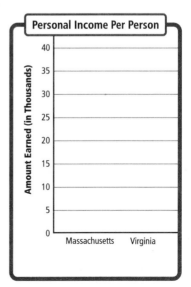

Personal Income Per Person

Amount Earned (in Thousands) / Massachusetts / Virginia

Practice Book
23   Use with *United States History*, p. 137

Vocabulary and Study Guide

Vocabulary

Write the definition of each vocabulary word below.

1. tariff _____

2. states' rights _____

   _____

   _____

3. sectionalism _____

4. Use two of the words in a sentence. _____

   _____

   _____

Study Guide

Read "Slavery in the United States." Then fill in the sequence chart below.

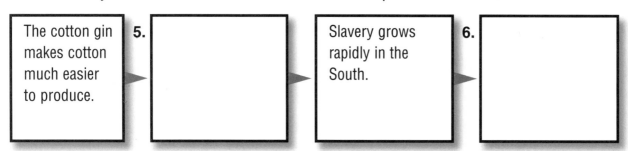

Read "North and South." Then fill in the compare and contrast chart below.

Region	Economy	Products
South	7.	9.
North	8.	10.

Skillbuilder: Compare Bar, Line, and Circle Graphs

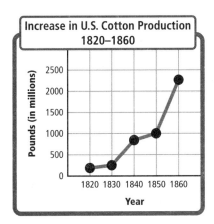

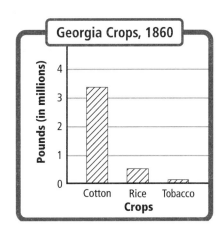

Practice

1. According to the bar graph, what is the difference in pounds between the cotton and tobacco in 1860? _____

2. According to the circle graph, which crop had the most exports in 1860? _____

3. What is the span of years on the line graph? _____

4. How are bar graphs, line graphs, and circle graphs different? _____

_____

_____

_____

Apply

Now use what you know about graphs to redraw the graphs. Draw a bar graph to show that the same amount of rice and tobacco were produced in 1860. Draw a line graph to show that cotton production decreased steadily from 1800 to 1860. Then draw a circle graph to show that the same amount of cotton, tobacco, and wheat was exported.

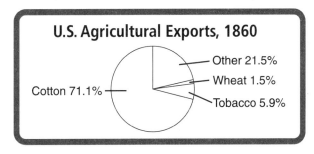

Vocabulary and Study Guide

Vocabulary

When you add a suffix to the end of a base word, you make a new word. Knowing a suffix and its base word can help you understand unfamiliar words. Look at the word *conductor*.

> Conduct "to lead or to guide"
> +
> -or "one who does a certain thing"
> =
> Conductor "one who leads or guides"

Break down the vocabulary word into its base word and suffix. Write the meaning of the new word.

> -ist "one who does something"
> -tion "the act of"
> -ism "the practice of"

1. Abolitionist = _____ + _____

Abolitionist means _____

2. Discrimination = _____ + _____

Discrimination means _____

3. Sectionalism = _____ + _____

Sectionalism means _____

Study Guide

4. Read "The Antislavery Movement." Then match these people to their identities by drawing a line between the name and the identity.

William Lloyd Garrison	printed antislavery newspaper, *The Liberator*
Frederick Douglass	spoke for abolition and women's rights
Sojourner Truth	spoke to white audiences about slavery

Vocabulary and Study Guide

Vocabulary

1. Draw a line connecting the vocabulary word to its meaning.

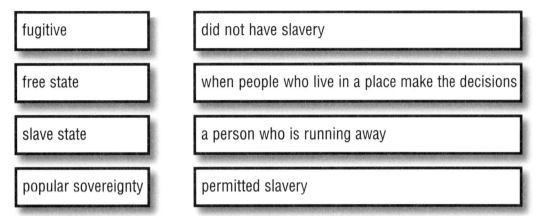

fugitive	did not have slavery
free state	when people who live in a place make the decisions
slave state	a person who is running away
popular sovereignty	permitted slavery

Study Guide

Read "Would Slavery Spread?" Then fill in the main idea and details chart below.

Compromise	What it did
Missouri Compromise	**2.**
Compromise of 1850	**3.**
Kansas-Nebraska Act	**4.**

Read "The Growing Crisis." Then answer the question.

5. What are three events that increased tension between the North and South?

_____

_____

Vocabulary and Study Guide

Vocabulary

Across

1. Seven southern states left the Union and formed the _____.
2. What southerners called for to protect their right to own enslaved people
3. Said to the South, "We are not enemies, but friends"
4. An issue dividing the North and South

Down

1. Began with the attack on Fort Sumter
5. President of the Confederate States

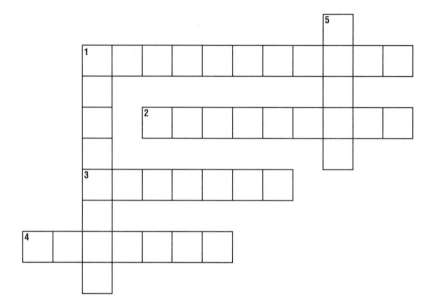

Study Guide

6. Read "Abraham Lincoln" and "Lincoln's Campaigns." Then fill in the blanks below.

   Abraham Lincoln was born in _____, but his family moved to _____ when he was a boy. Lincoln studied and became a successful _____. He was a member of the _____ Party. He also became a member of the Illinois legislature and later served one term in the _____. Lincoln argued against the spread of slavery, but he did not call for _____.

7. Read "Secession Begins." Then fill in the blanks below.

   Seven southern states decided to leave the Union and form the _____ States of America. The South Carolina state militia surrounded _____, which had U.S. soldiers inside. When President Lincoln sent _____ to the fort, the Confederacy fired on the fort with cannons. This was the start of the _____.

28   Use with *United States History*, pp. 164–169

Vocabulary and Study Guide

Vocabulary

Write the word for each definition below.

1. Slave states that stayed in the Union when the Civil War began

_____

2. Soldiers who are killed or wounded _____

3. When the army forces people to be soldiers _____

4. The freeing of enslaved people _____

Study Guide

Read "North Against South." Then fill in the comparison chart below.

	Advantages	Strategies
Union	Larger population; More factories and railroad lines	5.
Confederacy	6.	7.

8. Read "The War's Leaders" and "Turning Points." Then fill in the blanks below.

At the start of the Civil War, President Lincoln did not plan

to _____ enslaved people. Then

Lincoln made the _____ to weaken

the Confederacy. After that, the Civil War became a war to end

_____. In 1863, the Union won an

important battle at _____ and gained

full control of the Mississippi River. The Union also won the Battle

of Gettysburg, where President Lincoln later made a famous speech

called the _____.

Practice Book
29   Use with *United States History*, pp. 176–181

Vocabulary and Study Guide

Vocabulary

Write the definition of each vocabulary word below.

1. camp _____

2. home front _____

_____

3. Use the words in a sentence. _____

_____

_____

Study Guide

Read "The Soldier's Life." Then fill in the Venn diagram below.

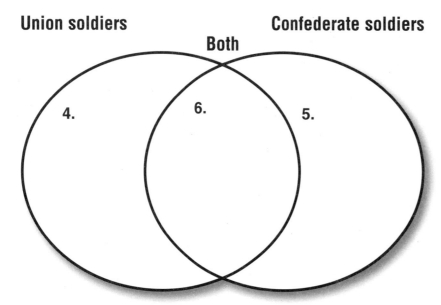

Read "On the Home Front." Then answer the questions.

7. Why did people in the North need photographs to understand camp life and battles?

_____

8. Why was life especially hard in the South during the war?

_____

_____

Practice Book
30
Use with *United States History*, pp. 184–187

Vocabulary and Study Guide

Vocabulary

Write the definition of each vocabulary word below.

1. telegraph _____

_____

2. total war _____

_____

3. desert _____

Study Guide

Read "Union Victories." Then answer the questions.

4. What two Union victories further weakened the Confederacy?

_____

_____

5. Why did General Sherman want to use total war on the South?

_____

_____

Read "Grant and Lee." Then fill in the causes-and-effect chart below.

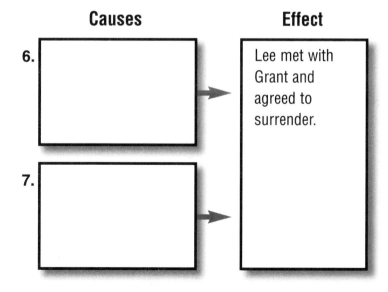

Causes

Effect

6.

7.

Lee met with Grant and agreed to surrender.

Vocabulary and Study Guide

Vocabulary

Across
1. Murder of an important leader
2. To charge a government official with a crime

Down
3. _____ Republicans
4. During Reconstruction, the South _____ the Union.
5. Southern states passed the Black _____.

Study Guide

6. Read "Plans for Reconstruction" and "Reconstruction." Then fill in the blanks below.

Before a plan for Reconstruction was agreed upon, President Lincoln was _____. _____ became President. Radical Republicans became upset because of the South's _____ and the election of former _____ leaders to Congress. Congress took control of Reconstruction, put the South under military rule, and voted to _____ the President.

7. Read "The Constitution Changes." Then fill in the blanks below.

Congress created the 13th, 14th, and 15th _____ to protect the rights of _____. These amendments gave the national government more power over the states. African Americans were granted full _____ and the right to fair and equal treatment. Some African American men became government leaders.

Skillbuilder: Compare Primary and Secondary Sources

> "A house divided against itself cannot stand. I believe this government cannot endure, permanently half slave and half free. I do not expect the Union to be dissolved—I do not expect the house to fall—but I do expect it will cease to be divided. It will become all one thing or all the other."
>
> —Abraham Lincoln, in an 1858 campaign speech to Illinois Republicans

Lincoln Becomes a Leading Antislavery Spokesperson

Americans began to learn of Abraham Lincoln's views on slavery when he challenged Stephen Douglas in the 1858 Illinois Senate election. Lincoln did not speak to outlaw slavery in the South, but he did not think the country could continue to be half slave states and half free states. He believed that soon the country would have to become all slave or all free states.

Practice

1. Is Abraham Lincoln's speech a primary or secondary source? How do

you know? _____

2. What facts do the two sources share? _____

_____

_____

3. What do you learn from the passage that you do not learn from

Lincoln's speech? _____

_____

Apply

Find a book that is an example of a primary source. Then find a book that is an example of a secondary source. On a separate sheet of paper, write a paragraph explaining how you identified each one.

Name ______________________ Date ____________

Vocabulary and Study Guide

Vocabulary

Write the definition of each vocabulary word below.

1. sharecropping ______________________

2. Jim Crow ______________________

3. segregation ______________________

4. Use two of the words in a sentence.

Study Guide

Read "Freedom and Hardship." Then fill in the causes-and-effects chart below.

Causes	Effects
Many African Americans became sharecroppers.	5.
6.	They formed the Ku Klux Klan.

Almanac Map Practice

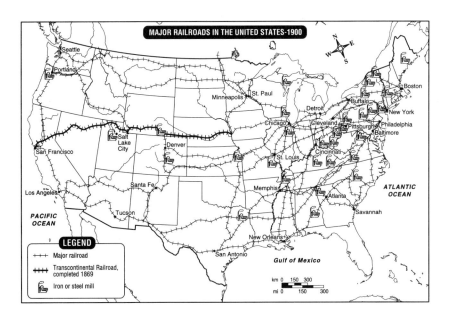

Use the map to do these activities and answer these questions.

Practice

1. Draw a line along the route of the transcontinental railroad.

2. In what city did the transcontinental railroad end?

_____

3. Where were most steel mills located? _____

4. Circle a symbol that shows an iron mill. _____

_____

5. What cities were near these coal mining regions?

_____

Apply

6. With a partner, plan a trip on a U.S. railroad route of the 1900s.
Choose a starting point in your state. Then choose an end point
somewhere else in the United States. Figure out which railroads you
would have to take to make your journey. Trace your journey on the
map. List the cities through which you would pass.

_____

_____

Almanac Graph Practice

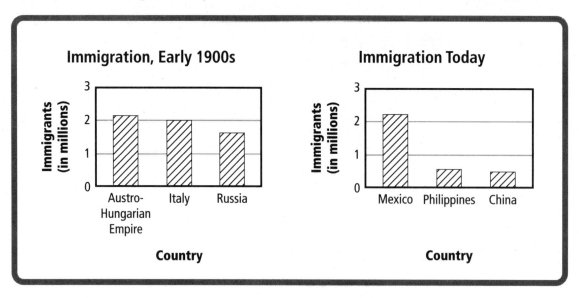

Use the graphs to answer these questions.

Practice

1. About how many people moved to the United States from Italy in the
early 1900s? _____

2. Have more people immigrated to the United States from Mexico or
Russia? _____

Apply

3. Complete the bar graph using the data in the chart below.

United States Immigration

Time Period	Number
1901–1910	8,795,000
1941–1950	1,035,000
1991–2000	9,095,000

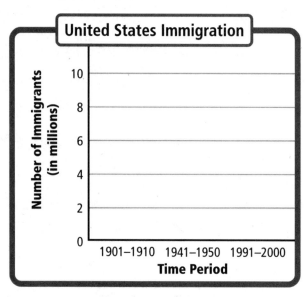

Vocabulary and Study Guide

Vocabulary

Write the definition of each vocabulary word below.

1. transcontinental _____

2. prejudice _____

Use each word in a sentence about the lesson.

3. _____

_____

4. _____

_____

_____

Study Guide

5. Read "The Telegraph Helps Communication." Then fill in the blanks below.

_____ invented the telegraph in 1844. The

telegraph used _____ and wires to send

messages very _____ over long distances.

Companies built telegraph lines that could carry

_____ from the East Coast to the West Coast.

The _____ helped bankers, war generals, and

reporters do their jobs better.

Read "The Effects of the Railroads." Then fill in the effects in the chart below.

Cause		Effects
The transcontinental railroad was completed in 1869.	**6.** →	
	7. →	

Skillbuilder:
Read a Time Zone Map

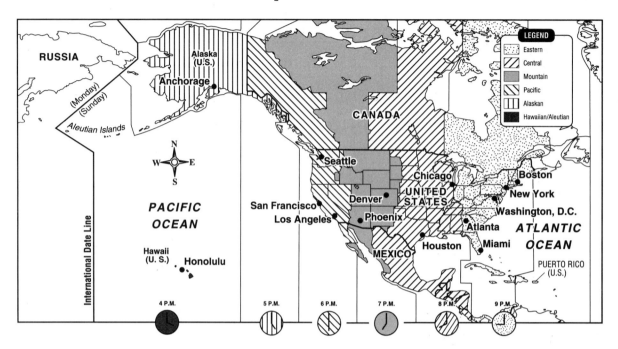

Practice

1. In what time zone is Seattle, Washington? _____

2. On the map, circle the U.S. city that is nearest to the International

Date Line. _____

3. As you go east from Chicago to Boston, do you add or subtract

one hour? _____

4. In what time zone do you live? _____

_____

Apply

Use your map skills to add more information to this map. Label the two
other countries on this map. Look at the region that is east of the Eastern
Time Zone. Label it Atlantic Standard Time on the map and on the
legend. Use a color or pattern to show that the Atlantic Standard Time
Zone is different from the other six time zones.

Vocabulary and Study Guide

Vocabulary

1. Draw a line connecting the vocabulary word to its meaning.

sodbuster	a settler's house and land
homestead	a long period without rain
Exodusters	the name for a Great Plains farmer
drought	African Americans who moved from the South to the Great Plains

Study Guide

2. Read "Settling the Great Plains." Name three groups of people who settled on the Great Plains after Congress passed the Homestead Act.

_____

_____

_____

_____

3. Read "Settlers Face Hardships." Then fill in the blanks below.

   Settlers found ways to adapt to the harsh _____

of the Great Plains. Trees were scarce so the settlers used sod to

_____. They also used new and improved

_____ to take the place of extra workers. Wheat

seeds from the East did not grow well in a climate with so little

_____, so Great Plains settlers tried wheat seeds

from _____, which grew very well.

Vocabulary and Study Guide

Vocabulary

demand	railhead	barbed wire	supply

1. Write each vocabulary word in the correct column.

Affected cattle drives	Affected cattle prices

2. Choose two words. Use each word in a sentence about the lesson.

_____

_____

_____

Study Guide

Read "Texas Cattle." Then choose the correct ending to each statement below.

3. Longhorn cattle were originally brought to Texas by

    A. cowhands.   **B.** vaqueros.   **C.** Spanish settlers.

4. In Texas, the abundance of cattle created a

    A. high demand.   **B.** low demand.   **C.** unstable demand.

5. In the East and North, the low supply of cattle made prices

    A. high.   **B.** low.   **C.** change often.

6. Read "The Cattle Drives." Then fill in the blanks below.

    The cattle drives only lasted for about _____ . Fences

made of _____ put up by new settlers on their land blocked

the cattle trails. When the _____ grew, ranchers no longer

had to drive their cattle hundreds of miles to reach a _____ .

In addition, many states passed laws to keep longhorns out because

they spread _____ to other types of cattle.

Vocabulary and Study Guide

Vocabulary

Read the clue and write the answer in the blank. Then find the word in the puzzle. Look up, down, forward, and backward. Look for bonus words!

1.	The area where an animal or plant normally lives or grows _____
2.	When an animal or plant is no longer existing _____
3.	To take in a new cultural group and change their culture _____
4.	A piece of land that the government has set aside for American Indians _____
	Bonus Words:

X	N	O	M	A	D	S	N	C	O
E	S	W	I	R	C	S	O	P	Z
B	T	T	O	Y	K	N	I	S	D
I	O	A	T	C	N	I	T	X	E
Q	L	T	L	K	U	L	A	E	T
U	A	I	B	I	N	U	V	H	A
W	F	B	I	O	M	O	R	C	L
W	F	A	P	R	E	I	E	X	O
A	U	H	E	V	N	N	S	R	A
U	B	I	V	A	T	I	E	S	H
N	O	S	D	G	A	F	R	V	A

Study Guide

5. Read "War on the Plains." Then fill in the outline below.

   I. Main Idea: _____

   _____

   A. Supporting Idea: _____

   _____

   1. Detail: _____

   2. Detail: _____

   _____

   B. Supporting Idea: _____

   _____

   1. Detail: _____

   _____

   2. Detail: _____

Vocabulary and Study Guide

Vocabulary

monopoly	strike	labor union	corporation	competition

1. As you read the chapter, fill in the details on the branching lines.

Big Business

Mechanization

_____

_____   _____

Study Guide

2. Read "A Time of Invention" and "Big Business." Then fill in the blanks below.

The _____ of the late 1800s improved life by

saving many Americans time and money. One of the most important

of these was the _____, which allowed factories to

stay open after dark. The new inventions helped businesses grow.

One business entrepreneur, _____, formed the

Standard Oil Company. Many people owned parts, or _____,

of the corporation. His company bought other companies, and it

became a _____.

3. Read "Workers' Lives Change." Then fill in the blanks below.

Businesses began using machines to make products and needed

many _____. The conditions in factories were often

_____, and the pay was very low. Workers tried to

improve their working _____ by forming labor unions

and going on _____.

Vocabulary and Study Guide

Vocabulary

Write the definition of each vocabulary word below.

1. tenement _____

_____

2. persecution _____

3. ethnic group _____

_____

4. Use one of the words in a sentence. _____

_____

_____

Study Guide

Read "Arriving in America." Then fill in the Venn diagram below.

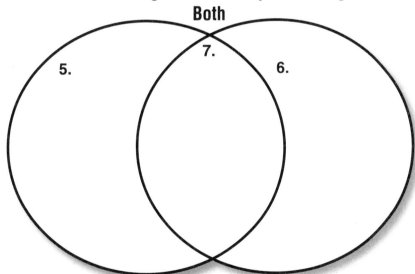

Asian immigrants   **European immigrants**

Both

5.   7.   6.

Read "Living in a New Country." Then answer the question.

8. Write two reasons why some Americans wanted to stop immigration.

_____

_____

_____

43   Use with *United States History*, pp. 266–269

Vocabulary and Study Guide

Vocabulary

If you do not know a word's meaning, try breaking it into smaller parts. It may contain a smaller word that you know.

Find the smaller words inside these words. Use what you know about the smaller word or words to write the meaning of the longer word.

	New word	Words in it that I know	Word meanings that I know	What I think the word means
1.	stockyard			
2.	skyscraper			
3.	rapid transit			
4.	settlement house			

5. Write the definition of *slum* below.

_____

Study Guide

Read "Moving to Cities." Then fill in the cause-and-effect chart below.

Cause   **Effect**

6. New _____ took jobs away from people on farms.   **7.**

Read "Changes in Cities." Then answer the questions.

8. Name two technologies that changed the way cities looked and worked. Give an example of each one. _____

_____

9. What made tenements unsafe? _____

_____

Vocabulary and Study Guide

Vocabulary

Write the vocabulary word that matches each definition.

1. Reformers who wanted to make new laws and improve society

_____

2. Someone who points out unpleasant truths _____

Use each vocabulary word in a sentence.

3. _____

_____

4. _____

_____

Study Guide

5. Read "A Time of Reform." Then read each description. In the box, write the name of the person described.

I was an African American writer and a leader of the NAACP.	I am →	

I gave speeches and wrote letters to lawmakers about women's suffrage.	I am →	

I started schools to give southern African Americans education and job training.	I am →	

I set aside land for national parks and worked with Congress to pass safe-food laws.	I am →	

45 **Use with *United States History*, pp. 278–281**

Skillbuilder: Identify Fact and Opinion

Practice

Read the following statements. Then identify each one as a fact or an opinion. Explain how you made your decision. Look at the steps in "Learn the Skill" on page 560 for help.

1. By 1900, Andrew Carnegie's steel company produced one quarter of all the steel made in the United States. _____

_____

2. Child labor was probably the worst problem the United States faced in the late 1800s. _____

3. It seems to me that the immigrants should have been treated better since they worked extremely hard in often dangerous situations.

_____

4. The inventions of steel frames and electric elevators in the late 1800s made the building of skyscrapers possible. _____

_____

Apply

Read "Making Changes." Write one fact and one opinion from your reading. Then explain why each is a fact or opinion.

5. Fact statement: _____

_____

Explanation: _____

_____

6. Opinion statement: _____

_____

Explanation: _____

_____

Use with *United States History*, pp. 284–285

Almanac Map Practice

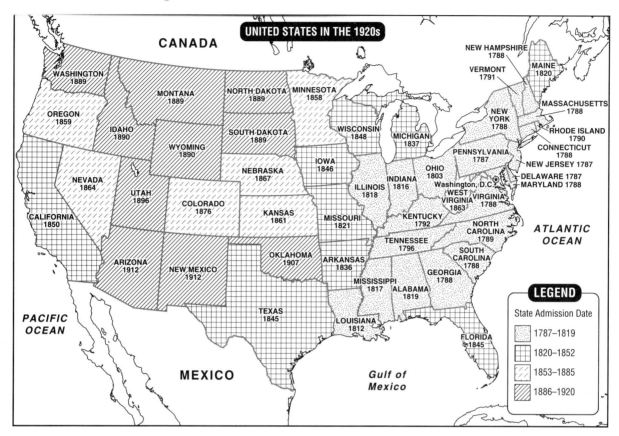

Use the map to do these activities and answer these questions.

Practice

1. In which year did the most states join the Union? _____

2. Circle the states that joined the Union in 1889.

3. Draw a box around the state that joined the Union in 1907.

4. Write the name of each state that borders the boxed state. Then list

the year in which each of these states joined the Union. _____

_____

_____

Apply

5. Work with a partner to identify the year your state joined the Union.
Then figure out how many states joined before your state and how
many joined after it. Note: Alaska and Hawaii became states in 1959.

_____

Name _____ Date _____

Almanac Graph Practice

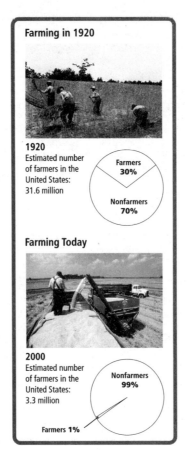

Farming in 1920

1920
Estimated number
of farmers in the
United States:
31.6 million

Farmers
30%

Nonfarmers
70%

Farming Today

2000
Estimated number
of farmers in the
United States:
3.3 million

Nonfarmers
99%

Farmers 1%

Practice

1. Were there more farmers or nonfarmers during the 1920s?

_____

2. What happened to the number of farmers between 1920 and 2000?

_____

Apply

3. Use the information below to complete the pie graphs.

1960	2000
Americans working in goods-producing jobs: 38%	Americans working in goods-producing jobs: 20%
Americans working in service jobs: 62%	Americans working in service jobs: 80%

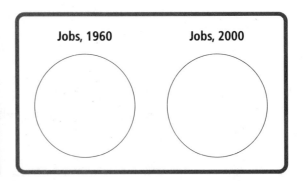

Jobs, 1960   Jobs, 2000

48
Use with *United States History*, p. 293

Vocabulary and Study Guide

Vocabulary

Write the definition of each vocabulary word below.

1. yellow journalism _____

_____

2. isthmus _____

_____

3. imperialism _____

_____

4. Use two of the words in a sentence. _____

_____

_____

Study Guide

Read "The Nation Expands." Then choose the correct ending to each statement below.

5. Alaska was a valuable purchase for the United States because of its

    A. mountain ranges.   **B.** fish, forests, and minerals.   **C.** gold.

6. Plantation owners in Hawaii wanted to

    A. stay in control.   **B.** give control to Hawaiians.   **C.** leave Hawaii.

Read "The Spanish-American War." Then fill in the seqence chart below.

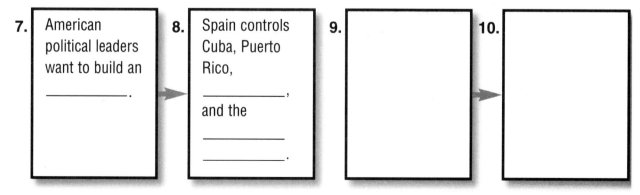

7. American political leaders want to build an _____.

8. Spain controls Cuba, Puerto Rico, _____, and the _____.

9.

10.

Vocabulary and Study Guide

Vocabulary

1. Draw a line connecting the vocabulary word to its meaning.

nationalism	An agreement nations make to defend each other
militarism	The belief that your country deserves more success than others
trench warfare	Building a strong military to impress or frighten other countries
alliance	When soldiers fight from long, narrow ditches

Study Guide

2. Read "Causes of the War" and "America Enters the War." Then fill in the blanks below.

Imperialism, nationalism, and _____ led to World War I. The Central Powers and the _____ were the two _____ in Europe involved in the war. World War I soldiers lived and fought in _____ on the battlefield. Most Americans wanted to stay out of the war, but when _____ began attacking American _____, the United States declared war on the Central Powers. Soldiers used new technologies, such as tanks, submarines, _____ dropped from planes, and _____ gas, for the first time.

Skillbuilder: Understand Point of View

"I am bitterly opposed to my country entering the war,...War brings no prosperity to the great mass of common and patriotic citizens...We are taking a step today that is fraught with [full of] untold danger...We are going to run the risk of sacrificing millions of our countrymen's lives."

— *Senator George W. Norris*

"We know that in such a government [as Germany's]...we can never have a friend; and that in the presence of its organized power...there can be no assured security for the democratic governments of the world...The world must be made safe for democracy."

— *President Woodrow Wilson*

Practice

1. Which speaker opposes U.S. involvement in World War I?

_____

2. Summarize Senator Norris's views.

_____

_____

_____

3. How might his job as President affect Woodrow Wilson's views on

entering World War I? _____

_____

Apply

Read about the effect of World War I on women in Lesson 3. Notice the quotation stating that the war helped women gain freedoms. Freedoms bring responsibility. For example, women today work as soldiers in the U.S. military. Do you think this is a good idea? Why or why not? Write a paragraph expressing your point of view on this subject.

_____

_____

_____

_____

Vocabulary and Study Guide

Vocabulary

Across

1. The 19th _____ gave women the vote
2. These people used less so soldiers could have more
3. Staying out of world events
4. Information used to shape people's thinking

Down

1. An agreement to stop fighting
5. Limits on the amount of goods people could have

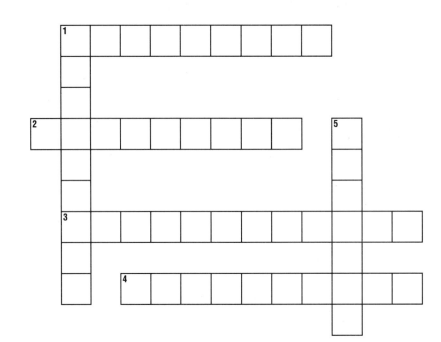

Study Guide

Read "The Home Front" and "The War Ends." Then fill in the chart below.

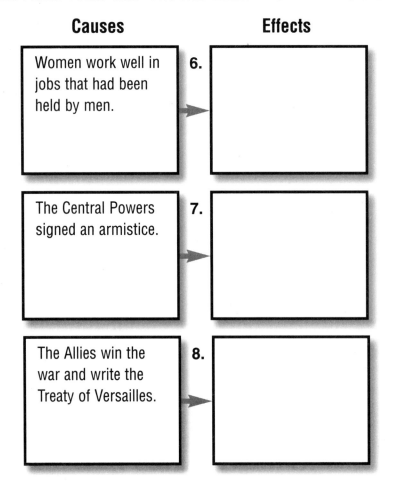

Causes / **Effects**

Women work well in jobs that had been held by men.	6.
The Central Powers signed an armistice.	7.
The Allies win the war and write the Treaty of Versailles.	8.

52   Use with *United States History*, pp. 312–315

Vocabulary and Study Guide

Vocabulary

Write the definition of each vocabulary word below.

1. boom _____

2. stock _____

3. stock market _____

4. division of labor _____

5. assembly line _____

6. Use *division of labor* and *assembly line* in a sentence.

_____

_____

Study Guide

Read "Changes in Production." Then fill in the sequence chart below.

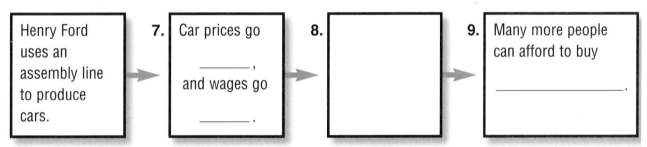

| Henry Ford uses an assembly line to produce cars. | **7.** Car prices go _____, and wages go _____. | **8.** | **9.** Many more people can afford to buy _____. |

Read "Government in the 1920s." Then fill in the comparison chart below to show how each President encouraged economic growth.

Calvin Coolidge	Herbert Hoover
10.	**11.**

Vocabulary and Study Guide

Vocabulary

Solve the clue and write the answer in the blank. Then find the word in the puzzle. Look up, down, forward, and backward. Look for a bonus word!

1. A program sent out over a radio or television station _____

2. A style of music that uses improvisation _____

3. In many cities, Prohibition led to these two problems _____

4. A person who flies an airplane _____

Bonus Word: _____

Z	E	L	I	O	Z	T	O
O	C	L	N	K	G	S	H
I	N	G	O	M	Y	A	T
D	E	L	E	Z	Y	C	R
A	L	I	T	C	Z	D	C
R	O	T	A	I	V	A	N
C	I	Z	E	J	E	O	J
E	V	Q	W	V	K	R	E
E	M	I	R	C	S	B	M

Study Guide

5. Read "A Changing Society." Then fill in the blanks below.

For the first time, women in the 1920s began to do things like

play _____, work outside the home, and go to college.

_____ music became very popular and America's

first _____ allowed people to hear live news and

music at home. Charles Lindbergh became the first person to

_____ alone across the _____.

Read "Problems of the 1920s." Then fill in the problem chart below.

Problem	Effect of problem
6. _____	7. _____

Vocabulary and Study Guide

Vocabulary

1. Draw a line connecting the vocabulary word to its meaning.

debt	The number of people who cannot find jobs
charity	A time when many businesses close and people cannot find jobs
unemployment	Money that one person owes to another
depression	A group that helps people in need

Study Guide

2. Read "Hard Times for Americans." Then fill in the outline below.

   I. Main Idea: The Depression caused hardship for Americans.

      A. Supporting Idea: The Depression was especially hard on farmers.

         1. Detail: _____

         2. Detail: _____

               _____

      B. Supporting Idea: Artists expressed the suffering during the Depression through their art.

         1. Detail: _____

               _____

         2. Detail: _____

               _____

Skillbuilder: Read a Population Map

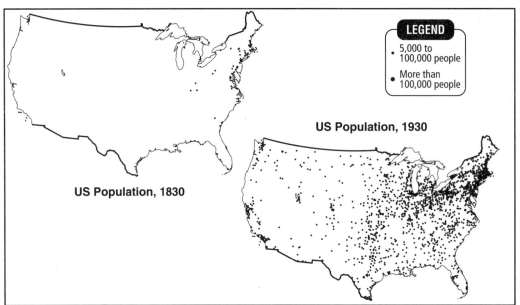

US Population, 1930

US Population, 1830

LEGEND
- 5,000 to 100,000 people
- More than 100,000 people

Practice

1. What part of the country had the largest number of people in 1930?

_____

2. Compare the two maps. Then explain how settlements in the United

States changed between 1830 and 1930. _____

_____

_____

3. Some places on the 1830 map have no dots at all. Does that mean

that no one was living there? _____

_____

Apply

Read "Hard Times for Americans" in Lesson 3. Look at the 1930
population map. How did the hard times affect the population of the
western United States?

_____

_____

Vocabulary and Study Guide

Vocabulary

Write the definition of each vocabulary word below.

1. hydroelectricity _____

2. Social Security _____

_____

3. regulation _____

4. Use *regulation* and *minimum wage* in a sentence.

_____

_____

_____

Study Guide

Read "The Election of 1932." Then choose the correct ending to each statement below.

5. President Hoover believed government should not try to change the

    A. business laws.   **B.** economy.   **C.** railroads.

6. Franklin Delano Roosevelt promised that his government would

    A. take action.   **B.** end regulations.   **C.** conserve resources.

Read "The New Deal." Then fill in the main idea and details chart below with details that support the main idea.

```
┌────────────────────────────────────────────────────────────┐
│ The federal government created programs called the New       │
│ Deal to help Americans during the Great Depression.          │
└────────────────────────────────────────────────────────────┘
```

7. ☐   **8.** ☐   **9.** ☐

Name _____ Date _____

Almanac Map Practice

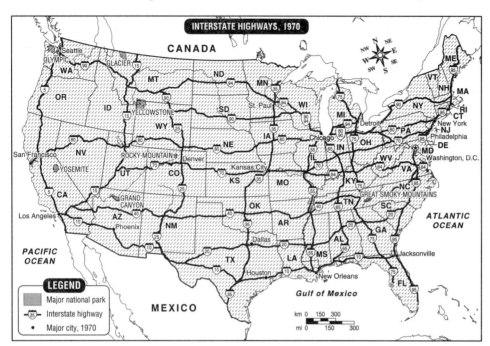

Use the map to do these activities and answer these questions.

Practice

1. Which interstate highway passes through Houston? _____

2. Use a crayon or marker to trace Interstate 80 from San Francisco to the city where it ends in the East.

3. Circle the city that is located at the intersection of Interstate Highways 25 and 70.

4. If a family living in Montana wanted to visit Olympic National Park,

   which interstate highway would they most likely use? _____

Apply

5. With a partner, describe two ways in which the Interstate Highway system has changed the way things are done in the United States.

   _____

   _____

   _____

   _____

Practice Book
Use with *United States History*, pp. 356–357

Almanac Graph Practice

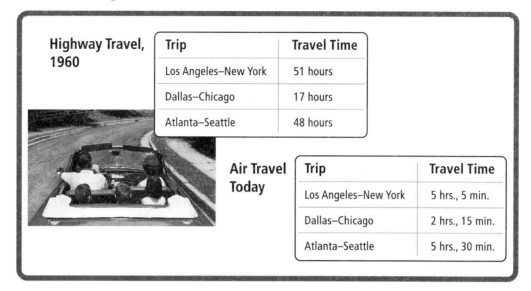

Highway Travel, 1960

Trip	Travel Time
Los Angeles–New York	51 hours
Dallas–Chicago	17 hours
Atlanta–Seattle	48 hours

Air Travel Today

Trip	Travel Time
Los Angeles–New York	5 hrs., 5 min.
Dallas–Chicago	2 hrs., 15 min.
Atlanta–Seattle	5 hrs., 30 min.

Practice

1. How long does it take to fly from Dallas to Chicago?

_____

2. If you wanted to travel from Los Angeles to New York by car in 1960,

how long would it take? _____

Apply

3. Use the information below to complete the bar graph.

Top Five Cities Visited by Overseas Travelers in 2003

City	Number of Visitors
New York, NY	5,714,000
Los Angeles, CA	3,533,000
Orlando, FL	3,013,000
Miami, FL	2,935,000
San Francisco, CA	2,831,000

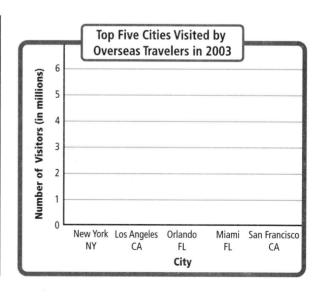

Top Five Cities Visited by Overseas Travelers in 2003

Vocabulary and Study Guide

Vocabulary

Solve the clue and write the answer in the blank. Then find the word in the puzzle. Look up, down, forward, and backward. Look for a bonus word!

1.	Adolf Hitler was this type of leader
2.	The idea that one race of people is better than all others
3.	When government controls the economy, culture, and people's lives
4.	The German, Italian, and Japanese alliance during World War II
	Bonus Word:

T	R	O	B	U	Q	M	R
M	A	L	L	I	E	S	O
N	S	I	R	C	F	E	T
E	S	I	V	D	H	X	A
W	I	Z	C	G	E	U	T
A	S	J	S	S	M	R	C
K	M	S	I	C	A	R	I
O	P	I	X	S	R	F	D
L	G	N	A	F	D	O	E

Study Guide

5. Read "Start of the War." Then fill in the blanks below.

The _____ ruined the economies of

many nations around the world. In Germany, Adolf Hitler and

the _____ Party took power. Hitler ruled as a

_____. He built a powerful military. The leaders of

_____ also encouraged feelings of nationalism.

Germany, Italy, and Japan began attacking other countries. They

formed an _____ called the Axis Powers.

6. Read "America Enters the War." Then fill in the blanks below.

At the beginning of World War II, President Roosevelt sent

supplies and _____ to Britain. He also worried

about Japan's plans to conquer other Asian countries. To try to keep

the _____ from interfering, Japan made a surprise

attack on the U.S. naval base in _____, Hawaii.

The next day, _____ declared war on Japan.

Skillbuilder: Analyze the News

ALLIES STOP SOVIET BLOCKADE

The United States and the United Kingdom are flying food and supplies into West Berlin to overcome the Soviet blockade. Earlier this month, the Soviets closed off all roads to West Berlin. Soviet leaders planned on starving the people of West Berlin until they agreed to become Communist like East Berlin. U.S. and British officials expressed their sympathy for the people of West Berlin and wished them well in their continued fight against the Soviets.

Practice

1. Is this a news article or an editorial? Why? _____

_____

2. How does the writer make you feel positive about one side and negative

about the other? _____

_____

_____

3. How might the Soviets have reported the event? Write a brief statement

of what happened from a Soviet point of view. _____

_____

_____

_____

Apply

Read about the eastern part of the war in "Battles in North Africa and Europe" in Lesson 3. Then write a short editorial about the war from the Allied perspective.

_____

_____

Vocabulary and Study Guide

Vocabulary

1. Draw a line connecting the vocabulary word to its meaning.

newsreel	To get ready to fight
mobilize	A place where prisoners are held during wartime
internment camp	A short film about current events

Study Guide

Read "Building an Army." Then fill in the main-idea-and-details chart below.

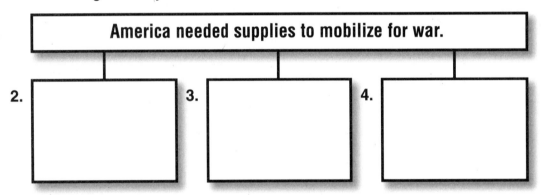

America needed supplies to mobilize for war.

2.

3.

4.

Read "At Home in Wartime." Then answer the questions.

5. Name two effects World War II had on American life.

_____

_____

_____

6. Why were more than 100,000 Japanese Americans sent to internment camps?

_____

_____

Use with *United States History*, pp. 370–373

Vocabulary and Study Guide

Vocabulary

If you do not know a word's meaning, try breaking it into smaller parts. It may contain a smaller word that you know.

Find the smaller words inside these words. Use what you know about the smaller word or words to write the meaning of the longer word.

	New word	Words in it that I know	Word meanings that I know	What I think the word means
1.	aircraft carrier			
2.	atomic bomb			
3.	concentration camp			

Study Guide

Read "Winning the War." Then fill in the chart and answer the questions below.

Event	What happened
D-day	**4.**
V-E Day	**5.**
V-J Day	**6.**

7. Name two military strategies the Allies used in the Pacific.

_____

8. What did President Truman do instead of invading Japan? Why?

_____

_____

9. What happened in concentration camps during World War II? _____

_____

Use with *United States History*, pp. 376–381

Vocabulary and Study Guide

Vocabulary

As you read the chapter, fill in the chart below.

Government controls production	People and businesses control production
1. _____ _____	2. _____ _____

capitalism	communism	command economy	market economy

Study Guide

3. Read "Roots of the Cold War." Then fill in the blanks below.

The _____ began in Europe as World War II came

to an end. The Soviet Union set up _____ governments

in much of Eastern Europe while Western Europe stayed

_____. The idea of the _____ symbolized

the differences that divided communist and non-communist

nations. To help stop the spread of communism,

non-communist countries formed an alliance called

_____.

Read "Conflicts in Europe Grow." Then choose the correct ending to each statement below.

4. The Soviet Union tried to take control of Berlin by creating

   A. an invasion.   **B.** a treaty.   **C.** a blockade.

5. The Berlin Airlift was an action taken by the United States and

   A. France.   **B.** Britain.   **C.** NATO.

6. The Soviets built the Berlin Wall to keep the people of East Berlin from

   A. receiving goods.   **B.** escaping.   **C.** traveling.

Practice Book
64
Use with *United States History*, pp. 384–387

Vocabulary and Study Guide

Vocabulary

Write the definition of each vocabulary word below.

1. arms race _____

_____

2. nuclear war _____

_____

3. anticommunism _____

_____

4. Use two of the words in a sentence. _____

_____

Study Guide

Read "Communism Around the World." Then fill in the chart below.

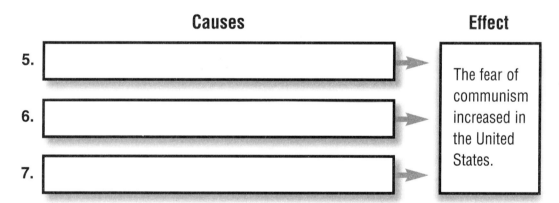

Causes   **Effect**

5. [   ]

6. [   ]   →   The fear of communism increased in the United States.

7. [   ]

8. Read "Cold War Conflicts." Then fill in the blanks below.

  When troops from Communist _____

invaded South Korea, the United States thought that the

_____ had helped plan the attack. The United

Nations sent in forces to defend South Korea. After years of fierce

fighting, neither side won.

65   Use with *United States History*, pp. 390–393

Vocabulary and Study Guide

Vocabulary

Across

1. Used to prevent polio
2. Eisenhower's campaign slogan was "peace and
   _____."

Down

1. A person who has served in the military
3. This device changed the way people learned about the world.
4. The increase in the number of babies born in the United States after World War II

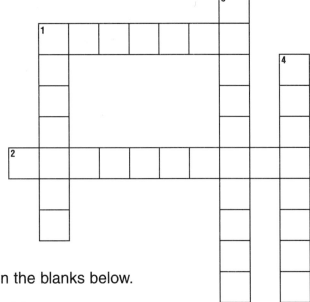

Study Guide

5. Read "Government in the 1950s." Then fill in the blanks below.

   President Truman worked hard to pass his _____

   laws. He proposed laws to build houses, help African Americans, and

   _____. However, many Americans did not think people

   needed help from the _____. President _____

   was a war hero. Under his leadership, transportation improved, and

   the U.S. _____ grew rapidly.

6. Read "Americans at Home." Then fill in the blanks below.

   The return of the _____ from World War II created

   a big boost in the U.S. economy. Many people started families.

   The _____ created a housing shortage, and many housing

   projects were built in the _____. People bought record

   numbers of _____ and other household items.

   _____ were improved and became less expensive to own.

   Dr. Jonas Salk developed a vaccine to prevent _____.

66   Use with *United States History*, pp. 400–403

Vocabulary and Study Guide

Vocabulary

1. Draw a line connecting the vocabulary word to its meaning.

desegregation	The rights that countries give their citizens
civil rights	A way to bring change without hurting anyone
nonviolent protest	Getting rid of laws that separate people by race

Study Guide

Read "The Movement Begins." Then describe what the people in the chart below did to help end segregation.

Linda Brown's parents	Rosa Parks	Martin Luther King Jr.
2.	3.	4.

Read "Civil Rights Victories" and "Gains and Losses." Then answer the questions below.

5. What did the Freedom Riders do? Why?

_____

_____

_____

6. What did Martin Luther King Jr. do at the 1963 March on Washington?

_____

_____

_____

Use with *United States History*, pp. 406–411

Vocabulary and Study Guide

Vocabulary

Write the definition of each vocabulary word below.

1. space race _____

_____

2. welfare _____

_____

3. generation _____

_____

4. Use two of the words in a sentence. _____

_____

Study Guide

Read "Kennedy and Johnson." Then fill in the chart below.

President Kennedy's programs	President Johnson's programs
5.	**6.**

Read "A Changing Culture." Then fill in the chart below.

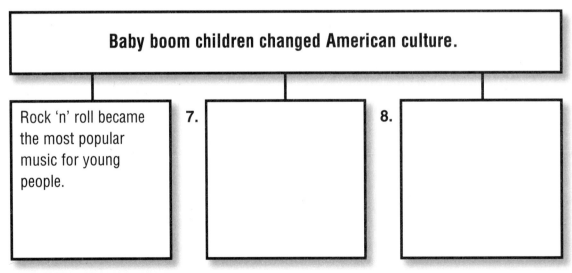

Baby boom children changed American culture.

Rock 'n' roll became the most popular music for young people.

7.

8.

Vocabulary and Study Guide

Vocabulary

If you do not know a word's meaning, try breaking it into smaller parts. It may contain a smaller word that you know.

Find the smaller words inside these words. Use what you know about the smaller word or words to write the meaning of the longer word.

	New word	Words in it that I know	Word meanings that I know	What I think the word means
1.	overthrow			
2.	cease-fire			

3. Use *demonstration* in a sentence about the Vietnam War.

_____

_____

Study Guide

4. Read "The Conflict in Vietnam." Then fill in the blanks below.

In the early 1960s, communist fighters called Vietcong

began trying to _____ the government of

_____. The United States sent supplies, advisers,

and _____ to help South Vietnam fight communism.

The fighting increased when the _____ army

joined the Vietcong. Even though the United States had advanced

_____ on its side, the fast-moving Vietcong soldiers

controlled most of South Vietnam.

Skillbuilder: Categorize

1. Look at the list of events below and categorize each one as a civil rights victory or civil rights loss.

Civil rights victories	Civil rights losses

- *Brown* v. *Board of Education*
- Montgomery Bus Boycott
- Birmingham Church Bombing
- "I have a dream" speech
- Civil Rights Act of 1964
- Voting discrimination in Alabama
- Assassination of Martin Luther King Jr.
- Other groups work for change

Practice

2. Which column has the most events listed? What conclusion can you

draw from the categorized information? _____

_____

_____

3. How might someone who is studying history benefit from categorizing

the events of the civil rights movement? _____

_____

Apply

Use the Internet or library to research six events that happened in the women's movement in the 1960s and 1970s. Then create a chart like the one on this page. Categorize the events as victories or losses. Think about what conclusion you can draw from the information.

     Use with *United States History*, pp. 428–429

Almanac Map Practice

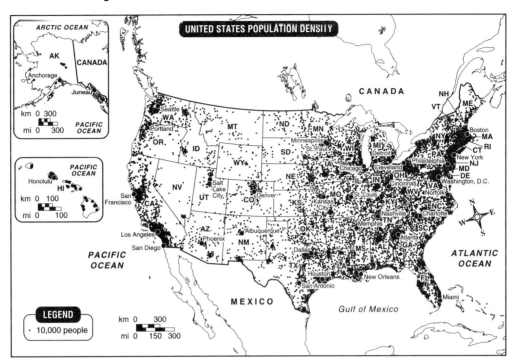

Use the map to do these activities and answer these questions.

Practice

1. How many people does one dot on the map represent? _____

2. Name the two cities in California whose populations seem to border

each other. _____

3. In which region of the United States does the population seem the

most dense or compressed? _____

4. Which state seems more densely populated, Alaska or Hawaii? How

can you tell? _____

_____

Apply

5. With a partner, study the "Electoral Votes" map in Chapter 18, Lesson
4. How does the number of electoral votes in California and Nevada
relate to each state's population?

_____

_____

Practice Book
71
Use with *United States History,* pp. 436–437

Almanac Graph Practice

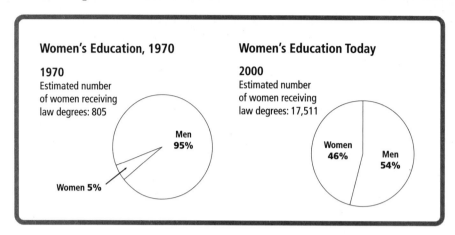

Women's Education, 1970

1970
Estimated number
of women receiving
law degrees: 805

Men
95%

Women 5%

Women's Education Today

2000
Estimated number
of women receiving
law degrees: 17,511

Women
46%

Men
54%

Use the graphs to answer these questions.

Practice

1. In which year did women receive more than 17,000 law degrees?

   _____

2. How much greater was the percentage of degrees received by

   women in 2000 than in 1970? _____

Apply

3. Complete the circle graphs using the information below. Draw lines to
   make sections in each circle. Write the terms *college* or *no college* in
   each section.

   In 1947, 4.7% of all women in the United States went to college for
   four or more years. In 1997, 21.7% of all women in the United States
   went to college for four or more years.

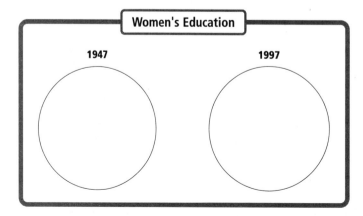

Women's Education

1947

1997

Vocabulary and Study Guide

Vocabulary

Write the definition of each vocabulary word below.

1. resign _____

2. accord _____

3. migrant worker _____

_____

Study Guide

Read "The Nixon Years" and "The Carter Years." Then fill in the compare-and-contrast chart below.

President	Successes	Problems
Richard Nixon	**4.**	**6.**
Jimmy Carter	**5.**	**7.**

Read "A Time of Change." Then fill in the category chart below to show the changes that came from each movement.

Women's rights movement	American Indians' rights movement	Migrant workers' rights movement	Consumers' rights movement
8.	**9.**	Some farm companies improved working conditions.	**10.**

Use with *United States History*, pp. 440–445

Vocabulary and Study Guide

Vocabulary

Write the definition of each vocabulary word below.

1. deregulation _____

2. deficit _____

3. coalition _____

4. Use two of the words in a sentence.

_____

_____

Study Guide

Read "Reagan Becomes President." Then answer the questions below.

5. What changes did Ronald Reagan make in government spending?

_____

_____

6. What led to the largest U.S. budget deficit in the 1980s?

_____

_____

Read "International Events." Then fill in the comparison chart below.

Event	Why it happened	Outcome
The end of the Cold War	**7.**	**8.**
The Persian Gulf War	**9.**	**10.**

Use with *United States History*, pp. 448–451

Skillbuilder: Compare Maps with Different Scales

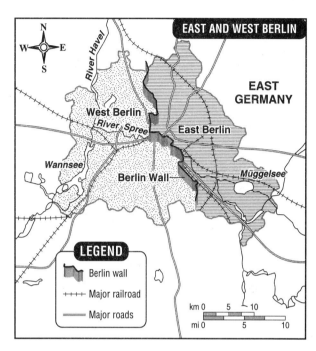

Practice

1. Which map shows a smaller area? How do you know?

_____

2. Which map would you use to find the distance from Hamburg to West Berlin? What is the distance?

_____

3. Which map would you use to find the approximate length of the border between West Germany and East Germany? What is its length?

_____

Apply

Describe a situation when you would want to use a map with a small map scale.

_____

_____

Vocabulary and Study Guide

Vocabulary

1. Draw a line connecting the vocabulary word to its meaning.

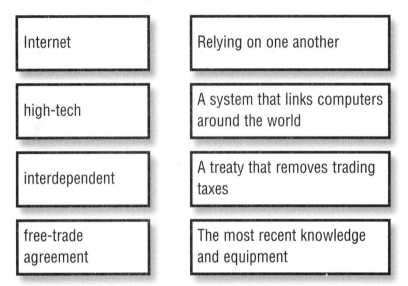

Internet	Relying on one another
high-tech	A system that links computers around the world
interdependent	A treaty that removes trading taxes
free-trade agreement	The most recent knowledge and equipment

Study Guide

2. Read "Clinton's Presidency." Then fill in the blanks below.

When Bill Clinton first became President, there was a budget

_____. Then the economy started to grow. By 1998, the

government had a budget _____. President Clinton acted

as a _____ in Northern Ireland and the Middle East.

During his second term, he was accused of improper behavior and

was _____. Later, the Senate found him _____.

Read "A Changing Economy." Then fill in the causes-and-effect chart below.

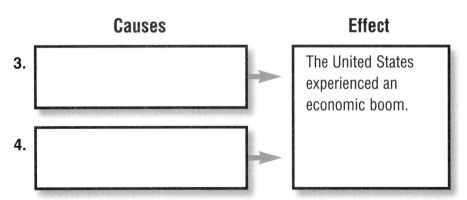

Causes	Effect
3.	The United States experienced an economic boom.
4.	

76 Use with *United States History*, pp. 456–461

Vocabulary and Study Guide

Vocabulary

Across

1. The vote of individual citizens
2. Democratic presidential candidate Al _____
3. Department of Homeland _____
4. Period of 1,000 years

Down

5. To become President, a candidate must win the _____ College vote.
6. Use of violence against ordinary people for political goals

Study Guide

7. Read "The 2000 Election." Then fill in the blanks below.

The candidates in the 2000 presidential election were George

W. Bush and _____. It was one of the

_____ elections in U.S. history. Although Gore

won the _____, Bush became President because

he won the _____. For the first time in United

States history, the _____ was involved in the

voting of a presidential election.

8. Read "Attack on the Nation." Then fill in the blanks below.

On _____, terrorists attacked the United

States in New York, Pennsylvania, and _____.

Thousands of people were killed. The terrorists had their

headquarters in _____. President Bush led a war

to capture their leader, _____. The United States

_____ the Afghan government but did not find

bin Laden.

Vocabulary and Study Guide

Vocabulary

Write the definition of each vocabulary word below.

1. province _____

2. multicultural _____

3. maquiladora _____

_____

4. Use one of the words in a sentence. _____

_____

_____

Study Guide

Read "Canada" and "Mexico." Then fill in the Venn diagram below to compare and contrast both neighbors.

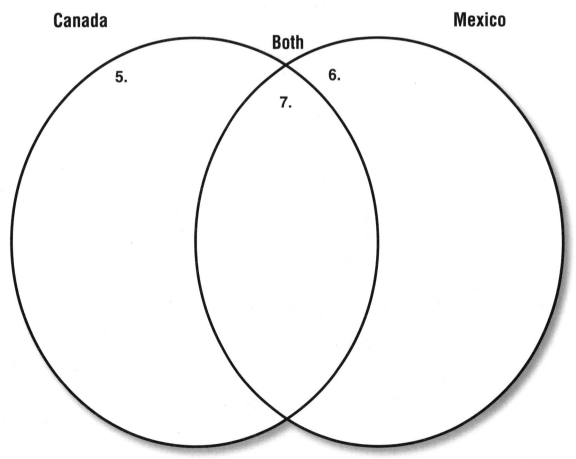

Canada

Mexico

Both

5.

6.

7.

78
Use with *United States History*, pp. 474–479

Skillbuilder: Resolve Conflicts

Keeping the Rio Grande Clean

The United States and Mexico share a border that is almost 2,000 miles long. About 1,000 miles of this border is a river called the Rio Grande. Over 100 years ago, both countries realized they needed to work together to care for the river. They needed to figure out how to solve boundary problems when the river changed course, and how to use the water.

In 1944, they formed the International Boundary and Water Commission (IBWC) to deal with water power, flood control, and rules that make sure no untreated sewage, or human waste, goes into the river. The United States helped Mexico pay for a new sewage treatment plant. Both nations want to make sure that the water they share stays clean for everyone.

Practice

1. What conflicts were the United States and Mexico trying to resolve?

   _____

   _____

2. What goals did the two countries share? _____

   _____

3. In what way did the United States compromise to make the solution

   work? _____

   _____

Apply

Use the library or the Internet to research a current conflict between two groups in your town or community. Use the steps in "Learn the Skill" in your book to identify the conflict and the goals of each side. Then suggest and evaluate possible resolutions to the conflict.

Vocabulary and Study Guide

Vocabulary

Solve the clue and write the answer in the blank. Then find the word in the puzzle. Look up, down, forward, and backward. Look for bonus words!

1.	"E pluribus unum" is an example.
2.	A person who escapes danger and seeks safety in another country
3.	Something that is passed down from one generation to the next
4.	A section of a country that is similar to a state
	Bonus Words:

E	R	A	P	O	Y	S	G
S	E	I	N	M	T	E	D
E	N	G	O	U	M	G	A
L	A	T	U	O	O	A	F
P	T	I	T	F	L	T	I
O	F	C	V	I	E	I	N
E	C	N	I	V	O	R	P
P	U	O	Z	W	M	E	K
N	O	I	T	A	N	H	B

Study Guide

5. Read "A Nation of Immigrants." Then fill in the blanks below.

    Some immigrants come to the United States to escape

_____ or to make a safer and freer life. Most

early _____ came from Europe and

_____. New immigration laws in 1965 made it

easier for people to immigrate from Latin America, Africa, the West

Indies, and _____. Many immigrants settle in

_____ with people from their home country.

6. Read "Many People, One Nation." Then fill in the blanks below.

    Most immigrants work hard because they hope to become

_____ in the United States. Their talents help

_____ the country in many ways. Ethnic and

religious _____ may be one of the United

States' greatest strengths. But all U.S. citizens, no matter where

they are from, are united by a _____ heritage.

Vocabulary and Study Guide

Vocabulary

1. Draw a line connecting the vocabulary word to its meaning.

responsibility	The process of learning the laws of a country and the rights and duties of its citizens
register	A person who helps other people without being paid
naturalization	A duty that people are expected to fulfill
volunteer	To sign up

Study Guide

Read "Citizenship." Then answer the questions.

2. What is the Bill of Rights? List three items written in the Bill of Rights.

_____

_____

_____

3. How else does the government protect the rights of citizens?

_____

_____

Read "Citizens' Responsibilities." Then fill in the compare-and-contrast chart below.

Responsibilities: adults	Responsibilities: young people
4.	**5.**